For

Lenny

my

Trombone

Buddy

Andre

41

MAGNIFICENT QUESTIONS

MAGNIFICENT ANSWERS

ANDREW JENNINGS DICKERSON

AJD

Magnificent Questions

Magnificent Answers

ISBN: 978-1-4634-1871-7   Hardcover

ISBN: 978-1-4634-1866-3   Softcover

ISBN: 978-1-4634-1865-6   E-Book

Library of Congress control Number: 2011911304

First printed 2012

The Magnificent Company
Deerfield Beach, FL

For you, The Reader:

*This is a magnificent book, expressing **21 magnificent questions, 21 magnificent comments, 42 magnificent answers** and **one mischievous answer.** The benefits being a guide, helping you to discover and*

Create

who you are

what you are

your purpose

power of choices

your own magnificence

the beauty of being in the Now

being happy (...if you want to be)

a healthier you, by choosing your reactions

clearer thinking, feeling and doing

nourishing decisions for yourself

peace in yourself

a knowing...and

anything you may want to know

Your presence,

is a present to

The

World !

Don't forget:

The

Best Way

to

predict

Your Future

is to

Create It.

...through

Your Choices !

*It is **always***

your Choice.

Isn't it?

This Book

is

dedicated to

My Mother and Father:

Margaret and Andrew Dickerson,

of Laurel, Delaware,

who Loved Me

and

I knew it !

Acknowledgments:

*I have had the honor and privilege of having
many, many people,
help me with this book during the past 43 years,
and to list all their names would take many pages.*

*Each of you, who has helped me,
know what you did and I want to say to you:*

*Thank you,
Thank you,
Thank you.*

Andrew J.

Magnificent Questions

The Beginning:

Several years ago, I presented corporate development seminars. After each seminar, several people would approach me and ask, " Who are you?" I thought, "What an unusual question!"

I never asked other people this question. It appeared to me to be such a personal question, discussing who I am. I didn't understand the purpose of this question.

Knowing we become what we think, I started to collect thoughts directing me towards peace, harmony, beauty, truth, and good health. I wondered, what kind of thoughts I had been expressing in my seminars creating a situation where many people asked, "Who are you?"

One day, I discussed this situation with a very close friend and he said, "Some people, in the seminars, feel your peace. The kind of peace that passes all understanding, and they want to know something about you. They want what you have".

So, I decided, if I wrote a book, I would save my time and their time by giving them my book, hoping it would resolve the question of "Who Are You?". But for years, I couldn't find the ideas and thoughts I wanted to express.

I was searching for ways to be simple, clear , interesting, and even entertaining.

One day I was re-reading Plato and his statement caught my attention:

THE QUESTION IS MORE IMPORTANT THAN THE ANSWER

Meditating on Plato's statement, it occurred to me to find a way to use questions to be the main subject. At the beginning of this project, I planned to create a book having only questions. I thought the idea of having only questions would be interesting...and it has been very interesting! It has opened many, many new territories to discover.

I presented these questions to two friends of mine, who happened to be clinical psychologists, and they both said they were more interested in the answers. I told them I could not give answers because answers change as we change, and because every person is different, the answers may be different for everyone. So, I thought about the situation ...and decided to present

MY CONCEPT, MY OPINION, OR JUST A COMMENT on each question.

Therefore, I am giving only My Concept, My Opinion, and My Comment, for each question and possibly some answers that have satisfied me. Also, comments, opinions, and concepts may be more interesting, especially knowing I will be traveling into unknown areas. I love to go into unknown territory, because the unknown expands my awareness, raises my consciousness, and brings forth a greater appreciation of the beauty of living.

Some of the comments or all of the comments may not satisfy you, and this is okay, because...
we are all very complex and very different.

And if you don't like, or you do like, my concepts, opinions, or comments, feel free to tell me. I am sure I will learn something, and I love to learn, hopefully in unknown territory.
Andrew

Magnificent Questions

Magnificent Answers

Question 1

What

Am

I?

A very important note:

A Reminder !

Before you start to read, I want to make it

very clear

I give...... O n l y

Comments, Opinions, Concepts,

and

Answers

that have satisfied me.

Hi, Today I chose

Question #1, *"What Am I ?"*

because it appears to me to be the beginning. A true genesis.

A Magnificent Question !

This question has given me a great opportunity to explore all the enormous possibilities of "What I Am", and my conclusion is,

<u>WE, as human beings, are the most</u>

WONDERFUL, MAJESTIC, and MAGNIFICENT

<u>creative force ever imagined!</u>

Our bodies alone are an amazing harmonic structure of design, engineering, and production. We are sheltered in an ideal environment with custom-made parts and a cooperative labor force providing nourishment all day. In addition, our magnificent emotional experiences create laughter, tears, joy, peace, beauty, love, and on, and on, and on!

As humans, we have created such amazing innovations as automobiles, airplanes, boats, telephones, televisions, and much more. We can project into the future, go into the past, or stay in the present. The greatest present we have is to be in the now... in the PRESENT!

WE ARE ALSO CAPABLE OF BEING, DOING, AND

HAVING,

ANYTHING WE CAN IMAGINE.

<u>*And this is*</u>

"*What I am*" and "*What you are*":

WONDERFUL,

MAJESTIC ,

and

MAGNIFICENT.

I think it would be healthy for me to think, to ponder, and to meditate about these things.

What do you think?

I think so, however, sometimes it sure does feel good
.....just to take off my shoes, turn on the television,
.....and eat my ice cream!

Andrew Jennings

The following

Answers

have satisfied

<u>Me.</u>

The roads we take will be different and this alone will guide us to different answers:

An Answer:

I

Can

Choose

My

Thoughts!

An Answer:

I

Will

Become

My Thoughts!

Question 2

Who

Am

I?

The time is now for Question # 2
"Who Am I ?"

Thirty-seven years ago, I realized ...
> *I did not know who I was!*

I knew some things about myself. For example, I knew I was very independent, loved nature, loved some types of music, loved to swim... but who was I really?

So, thinking about this, I wondered how I could discover the answer to the question

"W H O   AM   I ?"

If I went to a psychiatrist, it may take years and a large amount of money. In addition, how could I determine the level of insight and wisdom the analyst would have to help me achieve my goal?

Also, would I have the insight and wisdom to choose the right psychiatrist for me? Then I considered other analysts, such as a psychologist, and the same questions arose.

One day, as I was sitting under a large and beautiful tree, behind a small country church, observing a farmer plowing with a team of horses in a very peaceful and quiet area in the Amish country of Lancaster, Pennsylvania, a thought suddenly came to me out of nowhere:

Andrew, Andrew, Andrew!
Instead of trying to find yourself or seeking information from other people about "Who You Are", or trying to discover yourself... just CHOOSE the person

YOU   WANT   TO   BE !

WOW!

What a great idea. This is amazing. I can do that! I can really choose to be ...

WHO I WANT TO BE !

So I took a writing pad, wrote the subject at the top of the page. And within just 30 minutes I knew

WHO I WAS and WHO I WANTED TO BE !

It was magnificent and I felt so much joy in knowing I had finally solved the situation.

And,

so

I

decided...

THIS IS THE PERSON I CHOOSE TO BE:

Grateful	*Considerate*	*Sensitive*	*Generous*
Balanced	*Humble*	*Growing*	*Patient*
Kind	*Independent*	*Helpful*	*Wise*
Efficient	*Flexible*	*Receiver*	*Adaptable*
Speculative	*Explorer*	*Motivated*	*Helper*
Concerned	*Worker*	*Feeling*	*Warm*
Cooperative	*Trustworthy*	*Expressive*	*Objective*
Relaxed	*Stimulator*	*Trim*	*Liberal*
Conservative	*Genuine*	*Factual*	*Secure*
Adventurous	*Awake*	*Universal*	*Sedulous*
Ponderer	*Quiet*	*Insightful*	*Just*
Follower	*Easygoing*	*Loving*	*Knowing*
Trusting	*Committed*	*Harmonious*	*Positive*
Collector	*Prudent*	*In Tune*	*Musical*

Lyricist, Lyric Poet and Librettist

Honor Mom and Dad	*Honor My Children*	*Honor My Creator*	*Honor My Self*
Honor My Town	*Honor My Teachers*	*Honor My School*	*Honor My Friends*
Honor My Community	*Honor The World*	*Musical Arranger*	*A Traveler Mentally*
A Traveler Physically	*A Traveler of Unknowns*	*A Traveler Religiously*	*A Traveler of Water*
A Traveler of Science	*A Traveler of Psychology*	*A Traveler Spiritually*	*A Traveler upon Earth*
A Traveler Spatially	*A Traveler of Literature*	*A Traveler Emotionally*	*Self- Governing*
Keep My Word	*Social Anthropologist*	*Raise Awareness*	*Acquire Knowledge*
Acquire Insight	*No Intimidation*	*Grow Mentally*	*Grow Spiritually*
Grow Socially	*Grow Psychically*	*Grow Physically*	*Grow Emotionally*
Rest when Tired	*Raising Consciousness*	*Brush My Teeth...*	*...after each Meal*
Discerning	*Good Citizen*	*Competent*	*Risk Taker*
Paternal	*Philanthropist*	*Spiritual*	*Confident*

Caring	Neutral	Learner	Calm
Curious	Gracious	Sociable	Laughing
Humorous	Planner	Persistent	Reasonable
Punctual	Honoring	Listener	Thrifty
Play Violin	Play Banjo	Choosy	Pioneer
Microscopic	Telescopic	Nurturing	Free
Rational	Friendly	Enthusiastic	Meditative
Producer	Decisive	Nourishing	Alive
Teacher	Swimmer	Runner	Slow
In The Now	Ordinary	Responsible	Healthy
Song Writer	Poet	Moderate	Perceptive
Tenacious	Effective	Funny	Intense
Tranquil	Composer	Free Spirit	Accepting
Alert	Plain	Honest	Polite
Clean	Dreamer	Being	Nice
Gentle	Resolute	Practical	Natural
Thinker	Fast	Courageous	Persistent

Sprightly	*Resolute*	*Inquisitive*	*Organized*
Gentle	*Meanderer*	*Natural*	*Empathetic*
Focused	*Progressive*	*Passionate*	*Encourage*
A Project	*Practical*	*Fearless*	*Simple*
In-Harmony	*Creative*	*Athletic*	*Polite*
Expansive	*Artful*	*Open*	

Good Father,

Good Grandfather,

Peaceful,

Happy,

And...

To Live 137 and ½ years!

<u>Finally,</u> what a relief, what a new fountain of freedom I have discovered.

<u>Finally,</u> I can focus and put most of my energies into projects I have been desiring for years.

<u>Finally,</u> no more wondering "Who I Am".

<u>Finally,</u> I feel an inner peace that passes all understanding, an inner peace of knowing the possibility of

Great Beauty in This Life

It was a burden on me, not knowing "Who I Was", and I am sure it is also a burden on others who do not know who they are. So, if you want to copy my thoughts, feel free, you may want to add more or take away some. Whatever feels good to you, I believe you will discover

A freedom that passes all knowledge.

I am sure there are many more thoughts to consider, but right now, I think...

IT IS ENOUGH!

Choices.
Do you think these are enough choices?
I am inclined to believe so ...for the present.

Also, do you know what? I am still working on many of these choices, specially:

PATIENCE – HUMOR – LISTENING – GENEROSITY – GRACE

And now, after all of what has been said, I am tired ...and I deserve an extra large bowl of ice cream ...and I am going to reward myself by taking two naps.

Is this okay?
          Andrew

An Answer:

Some decisions are just

<u>too important</u>

to leave to chance.

*For
example:*

My Life.

An Answer:

I allow *Life*

to be a

Choice *or a* ***Chance***

...... and I live by ***Choice***

whenever I have a ***Chance.***

Question 3

Do

I

Know

My

Purpose?

Hi,

Today Question # 3 is ***"Do I Know My Purpose?"***

This one is really a whopper !

Aren't whoppers great? I just love them. Whopper ideas, whopper places, whopper trips, and whopper experiences. And I am sure you do, too. To be lost, confused, wandering, and wondering can be dynamic, frightening and enlightening. Most all of us are required to take these courses before we graduate from

" THE UNIVERSITY OF THE EARTH "

*For what reasons are you reading this? Is it possible you are searching for your purpose? Does it elude you? It may, and it may arrive at the best possible time. Or it may arrive when you least expect it. Either way, it will come ...watch **what** happens! ...It may be very interesting!*

It appears to me that this planet was one great constructive idea. The fact that this planet provides food, air, water, and shelter for human beings to experience is truly magnificent. This same planet also allows freedom of movement and freedom to express human emotions and adventures. Look at all the space we humans can explore and wander with hundreds of varieties offered in any direction we choose.

I cherish the feelings and thoughts I experience being nourished by the beauty of our planet. This benevolent planet has embraced us and is continually surrounding us with all of its being, (especially the ice cream) a huge understanding on its part.

We are all partners of this magnificent happening, and as naturally as we awake, we create our purpose each day.

Isn't it great to know we can create our own purpose each day, each month, each year? Of course it is, and we can create our purpose any way we desire as long as we don't hurt anyone, because to hurt someone will damage us and affect the entire planet in a destructive manner.

And we can do it being serious, having humor, being playful, or creating a healthier journey for ourselves.

So, have fun with this whopper!

DO I KNOW MY PURPOSE?

Yes, I do!

My purpose is to have many, many purposes bringing me:

Great Peace

Beautiful Harmonies

Many Learning Experiences

Joy in My Heart

Fun, fun, and more fun.

In my elementary school years, I wanted to learn all the lyrics to all the great country western songs sung by Gene Autry and Roy Rogers.

I also wanted to sing and play these ballads on my guitar. I loved it, and everything else was secondary ...UNTIL, I discovered symphonic music on the radio. I borrowed my grandmother's long knitting needle, turned on the radio for symphonic music, and used the needle for my baton. My new purpose was to conduct all the great symphonies in the world.

Everything else was secondary ...UNTIL,

I saw my hometown marching band of Laurel, Delaware, in the sixth grade. I knew I had to change my purpose because I wanted to be able to play all the musical instruments of the marching band. I wanted to hear all the different harmonies written for all the different instruments.

Everything else was secondary ...UNTIL, I started to play in big bands, playing the music of the Glenn Miller's famous orchestra. I felt a strong need to understand what was happening in this kind of music that made it so dynamic, complicated, sweet, and wonderful...

...UNTIL and...UNTIL and...UNTIL is still happening!

It seems as if I always took a bigger bite than I could chew, but it was always fun when I was chewing. And it would take another book to go into all the chewings between all the ...UNTILS.

I intend to continue my untils ...UNTIL, I reach 137 ½, and then I may decide to change, or not change my purpose.

Now, my purpose is to finish this book this year.
My purpose next year is to write my next book!

...UNTIL !

And now, my immediate purpose is to go to the fridge and get some good ice cream. Vanilla, Chocolate, Strawberry.
Any Questions?
Andrew J.

An Answer:

Questions guide

Explorers of Life

as

The Stars guide

Explorers of the

Universe!

An Answer:

When I choose to

Discover

a healthier life,

Wisdom

will hunger for

Questions.

60

Question 4

How

Will

I

Know ?

Sometimes a mystery appears such as

"*How Will I Know?*", *my Question # 4.*

However, there is no mystery with this Magnificent Question!

I can read about adventures, but those are another person's adventures. Not mine. I can go to the movies and see an adventure, and this adventure comes with sound. But, again, this adventure is another person's adventure. Not mine.

I can listen to a story, watch TV, listen to the radio, compute on the computer. But I think it best to create my own adventure, and the only way I will know about my adventure is simply to do it.

THE ONLY WAY I WILL EVER KNOW ANYTHING IS

TO EXPERIENCE IT, AND THEN IT WILL BE MINE!

I can see snow on TV, in pictures, and in movies, but the only way I can know snow is to see and feel snow in its environment: to touch it, taste it, smell it, roll in it, walk or run in it, slide on it, dig in it, sleep on it, eat it, eat snow cream, make snow balls, build snowmen and then watch them melt, be with and in the snow, or just "be within." Only in these ways will I ever know snow.

THE ONLY WAY I WILL EVER

KNOW

ANYTHING IS TO EXPERIENCE THE SITUATION!

Do I get it intellectually or just emotionally? It appears to me if we get information only intellectually, we don't have the whole experience. Nature gave us our emotions to balance our intellect. This is so important.

How will I know?

The treasure of knowing is one of the healthiest tools I have acquired. And I know there are many, many ways to discover this treasure and possibly everyone has a unique method of discovering the answers.

*****

I will share with you a procedure given to me many years ago by a dean of psychology at a large university in the United States. He was a very kind, considerate, and sharing individual. He shared the following procedure with me.

He said:

1. Write the situation or issue on paper.

2. Create an intellectual decision and write it on paper.

3. Then ask,
   "How I do feel about my intellectual decision"?
   - If it feels good, I go.
   - If it feels *uncomfortable*, I let my answer cook, or stew, or simmer until I know it is acceptable or not acceptable.

Sometimes it may take days for the answers, sometimes hours, or sometimes minutes, and sometimes only seconds.

I have used the above procedure many times and when I have super delicate situations to solve, I ask my Creator. And guess what? I sit and wait and an answer arrives.

One evening, I decided to create a musical composition without a title, subject, or theme by attempting to make my mind as blank as much as possible. I sat on a piano bench in front of my piano, and at the fourth hour, notes and answers came. I recorded the music, and the answer for the title was, " From Within."

A few years passed, and I played the composition for some musical friends. One said "You should title the song "From Within." This person did not know the same title "From Within" had arrived immediately in my mind after the music was written. Interesting. Isn't it?

But the most important concept was the fact I knew the composition was complete. There were no changes to be made, and there was a knowing it was finished. Knowing is a very good feeling.

Just simply knowing !

ANOTHER STORY:

One morning, several years ago, I took my car to a repair shop. While waiting for the repairs, I decided to take a walk around a shopping mall. I stopped for a moment and saw a lady with two dogs walk in front of me and enter one of the stores.

Immediately, the lady came out of the store and rushed toward me, and almost shouting said, "Who are you?" Having been confronted with this question many times, I quietly told her my name and said I was waiting for my car to be repaired.

She said, "Did you see those two dogs with me?"
I said, " Yes."

Pointing to the store she had entered, she said, " I own this jewelry store and the two dogs that you saw have been trained to warn me of any danger and protect me from any possible harm.

You are the only person I have walked near without my dogs making some small signal or sign to be alert. My dogs were very comfortable and calm in your presence, and this is the reason why I am curious as to who you are."

I said, "Well, their reactions confirm what I have been told by others. There is no hostility within me, and your dogs are extremely sensitive to pick up my vibrations of peace."

Some dogs don't have to ask "Who are you?"
They have a knowing and they let it be. Most dogs and I have an instant understanding because we are both knowing.

Andrew Jennings

And someday I hope I will have a knowing of when to stop eating big dishes of ice cream!

An Answer:

I know
the
Knowing
will
Come!

And

I know
when
the
Knowing
Arrives!

An Answer:

The Questions
may be Very Healthy

but

The Answers
may cause Great Pain

or

The Answers
may cause Great Joy

Am
I
Aware
My Choices
Determine
The Quality
of
My Life?

I love this choice for Question # 5

"Am I Aware My Choices Determine The Quality of Life?"

Here is an opportunity to express this Magnificent Question!

Many years ago, I read a book about the health value of oxygen in our bodies. According to the author, exercises, such as running, swimming, and biking were some of the best methods to increase the amount of oxygen in our bodies.

So, I chose to run almost every day, and when I exceeded three miles a day, I started to notice some days were easier to run compared to other days. I studied my lifestyle to look for any differences. Some days I would feel sluggish and heavy while other days seemed effortless and light.

The weather was about the same. My stress levels were about the same. My business and family were about the same. Then an idea occurred to me. There was one thing that definitely changed every day: the type and amount of food I consumed. I wondered if this could be the unknown factor. I decided to explore what would happen if I ate only one kind of food each day.

Immediately, the messages to my brain were very clear. Wow! this is fantastic. Foods altered my body immediately, so I learned to choose only the foods that made my running lighter and easier.

It was a huge awakening for me,
knowing my choices determined
the quality of my life
...and especially with my body.

It is very evident:

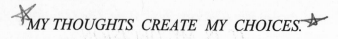

MY THOUGHTS CREATE MY CHOICES.

And it had been so simple to do. I said to myself, *Well, if my thoughts about choice of food is so dramatic, what will happen if I attempt to change my emotional thoughts?*

It didn't take very long to realize when I chose thoughts creating anger, resentment, road rage, impatience or any other negative thoughts, I got the message. I also got the message when I chose thoughts creating peace, harmony, love, or any other positive thought.

I looked at the world and ...

I realized the quality of my life is

***not** determined*

by my parents, my friends, my teachers,

my government, or anything in this world.

I AM IN CONTROL OF MY THOUGHTS,

IN CONTROL OF MY CHOICES,

IN CONTROL OF THE QUALITY OF

MY LIFE.

I still must practice quieting my mind, but I know, I truly know

✳ *IT IS MY DECISION*

and

✳ *IT IS ALWAYS MY CHOICE!*

Because it stops here, I'm going to change and have some beautiful peaches today, they look so good.
And then...another nap.

This always feels so good!

Andrew Jennings

An Answer:

Stop,

Look,

Listen, and

Think !

Discover what is

Better.

An Answer:

Thoughts, Deeds, Seeds

are much alike!

We reap what we think.

We reap what we do.

We reap what we plant.

Question 6

Do I

Ask

Or

Assume?

*My Comments for Question # **6*** ***"Do I Ask or Assume?"***

Oh, I love this Magnificent Question!

I have assumed too much. Too many times, with too many people, for too many years, and I will admit and share with you that no greater fool was there than I.

At times I have been too frightened, too intimidated, too humiliated and too uncomfortable to ask a question. But as I gathered more experience in life, I learned there was never a dumb question or even a small, stupid question ...UNTIL, it involves ice cream!

My asking was only a question, which was not smart, stupid, dumb, or intelligent. A question is only a question, and that is all a question is:

A QUESTION !

And above all, simply by asking - rather than assuming - I save a lot of time and a lot of grief, a lot of concern and a lot of undesirable feelings.   I learn so much!

Now, after many years, I just simply ask ...and ask ...and ask. And I find it is the answers that are dumb, smart, stupid, fantastic, and many times, hilariously funny and...

SOMETIMES WEIRD!

Andrew.

*And I am not as big a fool as I used to be
               ...except when I eat too much ice cream!*

An Answer:

Be Gentle,

Be Courteous,

Be Kind,

Be Curious.

and

Ask Many Questions!

An Answer:

Ask...

  and

    It Shall

    Be

  Answered.

Question 7

Do I Choose

to be

Happy

or

Unhappy?

Another Magnificent Choice for Question # 7 is.....

"Do I Choose to be Happy or Unhappy?"

WOW !   I bet you didn't know you could choose THIS ONE!

... DID YOU?

Well, don't feel so bad, because it took me over twenty years to discover this Magnificent Question. And you tell me...do you enjoy being around unhappy people? Of course not! Those unhappy people will tell you they can't help it, and guess what? They probably believe it. They have been playing the "PITY ME GAME" so long ...they don't know any other way to be.

They know they can choose to turn left or turn right; they can choose to stand up, sit down, or lie down; they can choose to speak or be quiet. In fact, they have the same choices as people who have decided to be happy. Interesting, isn't it? I repeat:

UNHAPPY PEOPLE

HAVE THE SAME CHOICES

AS HAPPY PEOPLE.

For me, I choose to be around happy people and leave the unhappy ones alone. I would never willingly fight a wild animal, walk toward a poisonous snake, or dive into an empty pool.
I realize I have all these choices, as do you. Isn't it great to know we can truly make these choices?

The choice to be happy and bring joy to our lives as well as the lives of others.

WHEN WE DECIDE

TO CREATE

HAPPY CELLS FOR OURSELVES,

THEN OUR SELVES WILL BE HAPPY !!!

Some years ago at a seminar I attended, the guest speaker highly recommended   *not to walk away   from unhappy,* negative, or miserable people.

He told us to ...RUN AWAY   **FAST.**

Andrew J.

Right now, I prefer to really, really run away and go to the store for some ice cream ...and some pumpkin pie.

An Answer:

Happy Cells

Create

Happy Selves...

An Answer:

Happy Selves

Create

Happy Cells...

An Answer:

And...

Mischievous Elves!

Question 8

Do I Live
in
Yesterday,
Today,
or
Tomorrow?

Being alive now, requires Question # 8

"Do I Live in Yesterday, Today, or Tomorrow?"

This question is not only Magnificent.
I believe it to be the most humorous one I know.

I know it will be very difficult for me to enjoy my breakfast this morning if I am trying to eat ...yesterday's breakfast or ...tomorrow's breakfast. I just don't know how to do this trick. I will also lose the appreciation of my breakfast, and I definitely do not wish to do this.

Being in the NOW is doing a WOW!

The sensations and the feelings brought forth are cleaner if not clouded or separated by yesterday and tomorrow. The clearest of NOW is the freedom of any other vibration, because the vibration of the present produces the greatest harmonies of body, mind, and spirit.

Just to recognize and feel the current of NOW is a beautiful experience of WHAT and WHO I AM, knowing there are no limits except the limits I create.

And...

TO EXPERIENCE THE GREAT QUIET,

THE GREATEST PRODUCER OF

GREAT CALM

AND

GREAT PEACE.

Which one do you think feels greater?

Laughing   yesterday, laughing tomorrow, or laughing now? I prefer to laugh NOW, because I haven't learned how to laugh yesterday or tomorrow. I haven't learned how to enjoy today, being in yesterday or tomorrow.

I believe, one of the greatest presents...

IS THE PRESENT !!!

What do you think?
                                        Andrew Jennings

And while you are thinking, I'm going to get a big slice of watermelon. I love it!
But, I don't have time for a nap today.

An Answer:

I

wonder

what

this

Experience

will t e a c h me.

An Answer:

It is always

My Choice

      to live in

      Tomorrow,

      Yesterday,

      or

      <u>Now!</u>

Question 9

Do I

Say

I Can

or

I Can't?

The rewards of history is Question # 9

" Do I Say I Can or I Can't ?"

Oh, Yes!

      I can say "I CAN." (and I can get ...into trouble!)

I like this story about Henry Ford, who created the great Ford Motor Company. One day, he asked two of his top men to come to his office. He asked each one if a certain project could be done. One said, "Yes," the other said, "No."
Both were right.

As a young man, I decided it was time to create and market an electric toothbrush. I went to an older friend of mine who was a graduate engineer of a large university. I asked him to help design and create an electrical tooth brush. He said: "Not a good idea. Nobody will buy it." Guess what? I believed him, and ten years later I saw an electrical toothbrush in a store.

NEVER AGAIN DID I EVER ALLOW NEGATIVE PEOPLE

TO INFLUENCE ME,

ESPECIALLY EXPERTS !

Many times I have defeated myself before I even started by saying, "I don't know how to do this," "It's too difficult," or "It can't be done." And on, and on, and on. Then, somehow, a thought came to me: "Perhaps I don't know, but one thing for sure is the fact that if I do not make an attempt, I will never know." So, I adopted the idea,

"Perhaps I don't know, but let's see what happens if

I make an attempt."

The "LET'S SEE WHAT HAPPENS" thought has helped immensely! Even when I fall on my face, or other people say I am nuts or my idea is impractical, I meditate and say, "Let's explore this situation, because it is only a learning experience.

One of my best learning experiences was several years ago when I planned a trip taking the southern route to California from Delaware to visit some friends. I purchased a used car. It was an older model and did not have air conditioning.

Now, I wasn't going to take the southern route, in the summer, with four children and two parents without air conditioning. So, when it was time, I inquired how to put an air conditioner unit in this car.

I was surprised when I went to three auto air conditioning businesses, and all three shops told me it could not be done on this particular car. But I was determined to take this trip with air conditioning. What was I to do?

I had met an intelligent auto mechanic recently in my endeavors to recondition the car, so I decided to see him.

I asked, "Have you ever had any experience putting air conditioning units in automobiles?"

He said, "No."

I said, "Good, because together we are going to find a way to install an air conditioning unit in my car.

He said: "Okay"

(I felt sooo good hearing this positive statement!
What a relief!

I read the installation manual, kept asking questions, and within three hours, the air conditioning unit was installed and worked great for the whole trip.

Today, I still listen to experts, and when they say no, I have a habit of talking with people who have the skills and tools to accomplish...What some experts don't know:

An Attitude of " I CAN."

The experiment on the attempt to start a project is only *a learning experience,* that's all, no big deal.

How will I ever know if I don't do it ? The universe is going to unfold the way it decides. So...

LET'S GO ! ... DO IT !

I BELIEVE I CAN ! ...LETS SEE WHAT HAPPENS !

What do you think?
Andrew J.

I think it is time for some beautiful blueberries, they look sooooo good today, and a bigger slice of watermelon and, Oh, yes ...a nap!

An Answer:

To The Universe,

I do not say, ...

"I want.

I say, ...

"Thank you."

An Answer:

Humor

and

Persistence

are my best

F r i e n d s.

Question 10

Do I

Focus

on

The Situation

or

The Solution?

*Choosing will change everything, especially Question # **10**,*

"Do I *Focus* on *The Situation* or *The Solution?*"

I remember one philosopher saying:

"The trouble with most people is the fact people don't have enough problems."

WOW! What a different attitude!

However, fortunately, I have learned this statement is true.

THE MORE PROBLEMS I HAVE , THE MORE I WILL LEARN.

AND THE LARGER THE PROBLEM I HAVE,

THE MORE I WILL LEARN.

So, some years ago, I asked my Creator to give me big problems, and to give me many problems, knowing I will learn more. Well, I got them, big ones, and a lot of them, until one day I told my Creator to ease up. I had too many at the time. It was too stressful. Then I started to have a distaste for problems...

UNTIL... I found a better and healthier attitude.

A problem equaled a negative force, so I decided to get rid of the negative force by substituting the concept of having only situations to solve. The word "situation" is neutral to me, so now I no longer have problems, only...

"SITUATIONS TO SOLVE."

I had an interesting experience with two psychologist friends when both of them asked, " Andrew, how come you don't bring your problems to us? Surely you have problems."

I answered, "Problems?

Why would I want problems?

I have discovered they are not healthy for me. I only have situations to solve, and I need to practice, so I can improve myself. I don't want to bother you with my situations. Besides, if you solved my situations for me, I might grow lazy, and that is not healthy.

Also, I would have lost

"THE OPPORTUNITY OF HAVING A NEW EXPERIENCE"

So, I go a step farther by focusing on solutions. I have discovered that when I spend my time on solutions, answers come faster. They are clearer and they are very often very interesting.

Knowing...

I CAN CHANGE ANY SITUATION BY CHANGING

MY THOUGHTS .

... and it is through the many solutions that I really learn.

... and I prefer the larger situations to solve as I will expand my mind to a larger experience.

Sometimes, I come up with some nutty solutions, (perhaps because I have always enjoyed eating nuts). Now I focus on nutty solutions and I am often surprised how interesting the answers change, and can be entertaining and full of nutty surprises.

SOMETHING TO CONSIDER:

If you were taking a boat trip across an ocean and you had the choice of a captain who had survived big storms, turbulent waters, and other dangerous episodes, or a captain who had only sailed in calm waters, which captain would you choose?

And I am choosing to take a long walk today instead of a nap. I love to do this too!

ANOTHER TRUE STORY:

Another friend asked, " Andrew, how come you never tell me any of your problems, like my other friends?" I looked at him, chuckled a little, and said: "Why would I want problems, they are not healthy. I only have situations to solve." He shook his head and said, " You are nutty."

I agreed and said, "I really love nuts. I had some yesterday. Black Walnuts. They are my favorite nut and favorite food."

ANOTHER METHOD I USE TO SOLVE SITUATIONS :

First, ... I write the Situation on a pad:

"I DO NOT KNOW WHAT TO DO"

Then, ... I write two lists: FOR and AGAINST:

FOR:	AGAINST:
List the Positives.	List the Negatives.
1. It looks good.	1. It looks not so good.
2. It feels good.	2. It feels not so good.
3. It tastes good.	3. It tastes not so good.
4. It sounds good.	4. It sounds not so good.
5. My mother says it is good.	5. My father says it is not so good.

DECISION: I am going to do it!

Mother is always right !!!

THE MOST IMPORTANT QUESTION IS:

<u>*How Do I Feel about the Decision ?*</u>

      And   *If I feel good……I do it !*

      And   *I f I don't feel good……I don't do it !*

"THE ORCHESTRA-LEADER SITUATION"

I was fifteen years young, in the 10th grade in a beautiful public school, and I had been elected president of the student council. In order to raise money for the council, we decided to sponsor a dance for the students, hoping to make enough money to pay the orchestra and have some left over to achieve our goal.

Near the end of the dance, I went to the table where students had collected the money and, to my disappointment, discovered there was not enough money to pay the orchestra. I was very concerned about this situation. I went to the principal, who was the chaperone that evening, and asked him what we should do about the insufficient funds.

He said, " You are the president," and then turned, walked away, ……and left the building. He left me standing alone in the hallway!

As I stood there watching him leave the building, I thought, "Well, isn't that something? He left me stranded. What will I do? I am so embarrassed. What will the orchestra leader do when I approach him? How angry will he be?"

I really wanted to leave and go home, but I knew the situation would still be there tomorrow, and I would have to face it then, and the situation might be even worse. I would appear as a coward, but most of all, it would reveal me as being irresponsible.

I was scared, nervous, and anxious about the situation. I could let myself down, but not the school and all the faith the students had in me to represent them.

So, the moment when the last dance was finished, I went to the orchestra leader and told him the situation of not having enough money to pay him tonight. He said, "Don't worry. It happens many times. Just send what you owe when you have the money."

I was sooooo relieved. What a nice person!

He understood my problem, he was not upset, and I had gone through an unnecessary emotional upheaval. What a terrific lesson! I remembered this lesson, when similar situations arrived in my life.

ANOTHER TRUE STORY:

Once, in my last semester at the university, I didn't have the money necessary to pay for my room and board. Pondering the situation, I remembered the lesson from

"The Orchestra-Leader Situation."

Feeling anxious and not very comfortable, I went to the accounting department at the university and told them about my situation. They said, "Don't worry. Pay on a monthly basis and, if you can't, pay us when you can." What nice people, and they were so understanding! I had experienced the same anxious feeling, which again had been unnecessary.

ANOTHER TRUE STORY:

At another time in my life, when family expenses were extremely high, I was informed my daughter would not be able to continue her senior year at her university until I paid the entire amount of the tuition. Another very anxious time, but again...

I remembered "The Orchestra-Leader Situation"

I called the president of the university and told him the situation, but I also had to tell him I did not know when I could pay, and the debt was a lot of money, in the thousands.

He said," Don't worry. Pay when you can. Just tell your daughter when she arrives at the university this fall to go directly to the comptroller and tell him the situation. The situation will be resolved. Pay us when you can."

I thought, What a nice man. What a great relief!
And again, life revealed to me, the anxious feeling was unnecessary.

Having been in the business world for many years and having been the president of many, many companies, I realize what a terrific lesson I received from my principal when he said to me:

"You are the president"

... and he walked away ...

This taught me ...

I AM

THE SOLUTION

AND

ALWAYS

THE SOLUTION

Andrew

By the way, ...I'm fasting today.

An Answer:

I know

My

Questions

can create many

Alternatives

to every

Situation.

An Answer:

I

never,

n e v e r,

never give up.

Except to common

sense.

Do I

See and Feel

Things

<u>as they are</u>

...or as

I Am ?

The Truth is for Question # 11.

"Do I See and Feel Things As They Are ...or As I Am?"

WOW ! This is clearly a most Beautiful Question!

We know when we use a camera to take pictures, if the lens is not in focus, the pictures will not be in focus. In fact, the pictures will look distorted, weird, and sometimes funny. We will never, ever, ever get a good picture.
A picture that is clear, clean, in balance, and especially true.

When we feel anger, jealously, or any other negative emotional disturbance, we cannot see or feel things as they are. Alcohol, drugs, and other addictions will create many distortions, and we will not see, hear, feel, or know the truth.

I will never forget, as a young boy, the fear penetrating me after I saw a motion picture titled, "The Mummy's Hand." I had a chore, while living on a farm, of closing the doors of my grandmother's chicken house, which was about a quarter mile from the house. And guess what? I saw the mummy's hand after me every night!

It never got me, because I ran so fast. (In fact, it was just about impossible for anything to catch me.) But I knew the mummy's hand was there every night trying to catch me. I guess I figured one way to get rid of the mummy's hand was to keep running until it got tired of chasing me. In fact, I can still see it today! It did leave me, but I never forgot it.

Any form of disturbance may cause me to be out of balance, not in
focus, unclear, and unable to see, hear, feel, or know the truth!

My grandmother's sweet potato pie looked exactly like pumpkin pie, but it sure did not taste as good as pumpkin pie.

You see, her pie looked exactly like pumpkin pie, so I expected it to taste like pumpkin pie. What a disappointment!

Being disappointed, we will not be able to see things as they are. We surely will not be able to see, hear or feel a clear picture ...until we are in balance, in tune, and feeling great peace.

Many of us need eyeglasses in order to see things in a clearer perspective. Without these eyeglasses, we would live in a distorted and foggy world; we would not be able to see things as they are, but as we are. Similar to a camera not in focus, the picture would not be clear.

*It appears to me, many of us (especially me), need intellectual and emotional glasses in order to think, see and feel things as they really are, **not** as we are -in order for us **to be** more aware, more understanding, less judgmental, and more appreciative of what we are.*

A friend once told me he was more interested in

WHAT IS RIGHT

rather than

WHO IS RIGHT

I forgot this instruction many times as I erroneously considered myself right. Thoughts do not always manifest into things, feelings are not always facts, and we are only humans falling and walking, learning and forgetting.

Each of us takes a different path, seeing a world different from others. Each one of us is definitely different.

Interesting, isn't it?

ANOTHER STORY:

I remember as a young child of seven years, our kitchen seemed to be a very large room. When I revisited the same kitchen thirty years later, the room seemed much smaller. Of course, I had doubled my weight and doubled my height, but the kitchen size had remained the same. I had changed, immensely, while the kitchen had remained the same.

My perception and feelings had changed, but ...the kitchen had not changed.

Some of us are nearsighted, some farsighted, some of us need eyeglasses to correct our inability to see objects as they truly are. Without these eyeglasses, we would live in a distorted and possible fogged world, far from the truth and far from what it is.

Just as pictures taken with an out-of-focus camera will be blurry, distorted, and unclear, the things I think, feel, hear and see when I get out of tune, out of balance, out of whack will not be the truth.

This is when subjectivity appears.

THE TRUE OBJECTIVITY HAS BEEN LOST

AND WILL NOT RETURN

...UNTIL,

I BECOME IN BALANCE, IN TUNE,

AND FEEL GREAT PEACE

Many, many times in my life, I was out of balance and I did not know it. Guess what happened? I lost my perception of being objective, and made many errors. I missed the mark, and even though it was only a learning experience.

I had lost the beauty of having the truth.

Thoughts do not always manifest into things. Feelings are not always facts. Many times our behavior is based on things as we are, not as things truly are.

I love this Thought:

"IT IS HEALTHIER TO BE UNDERSTANDING

THAN TO BE UNDERSTOOD"

What do you think ?

Andrew Jennings

My perceptions are going to change rapidly today.
I am going to have a carrot, lettuce, and a tomato instead of nuts or ice cream.

An Answer:

Are My Fears

Real or Imagined?

Questions

Discover

The Truth!

An Answer:

All my

Answers

Are

Within Me.

Question 12

Am I Doing

what

I

Love

To Do?

My desires chose Question # 12

"Am I Doing What I Love to Do?"

Many years ago, I decided that one of the most healthy adventures I could create, would be to do only the things I loved to do. It took several years to solve this situation. I found part of the solution when I was in my teens, but I didn't solve it completely ...UNTIL, I attended *my own funeral.* (I learned this powerful technique from a friend of mine.)

I fantasized being placed in a casket and lowered into the ground. I watched my family and friends walk by, each one looking at my casket. Ten years go by, and only a few of my family come to look at my gravesite. Fifty years go by, and no one comes anymore.

While I was asleep, I thought about what I had missed and what I would have really enjoyed doing if I hadn't died. When I awoke, I realized I could leave my gravesite and enter the world again.

WOW! This time, knowing what I had missed and knowing what I loved to do, I moved joyfully into all the unknown areas I wanted to experience. There were many, many things I wanted to experience. I wanted to:

1. -**Study classical piano** until I knew I had been fairly fed. I wanted to play Bach, Beethoven, Gershwin and me. I did some composing while playing in restaurants with a good grand piano.

It was funny. People had no idea what was happening. I was practicing scales, playing my music, and having a lot of fun. I enjoyed playing for singers in nightclubs. It was always so different with each singer, and I really had to stay alert and be willing to take musical risks.

Human nature is so moving and touching to me at times, especially the manner in which the owners of the restaurants fired me. The owners were never there. It was always on their night off and the bartender gave it away when he had difficulty looking me in the eye. After my last song, the bartender or manager would come to me with my pay and say, "Sorry, I have to tell you this is your last night to play".

I felt sorry for them, but never for me. A new job and a new experience were just around the corner.

2. -Study classical trombone. *And, WOW, this was some great trip! My trombone teacher said, "The only thing I can teach you is ...*

" TO BE MORE AWARE"

No teacher had ever said this to me, and I realized this is what teachers really do. They teach us to be more "AWARE." Another beautiful present on this planet!

ISN'T IT GREAT TO KNOW

OUR TEACHERS ARE BEAUTIFUL PRESENTS,

......AND PRECIOUS GIFTS ?

I was in heaven studying piano and trombone at the same time, devoting ten to twelve hours a day in music.

I think we need more Piano and Trombone Teachers in the World !!!

3. -Read The great Ideas Program. *I had earned a set with over fifty-five volumes to read, and I took the time to be fed intellectually*

*4. Take time -**To heal my emotional wounds** and search for spiritual values.*

*5. -**Study man-made laws** at the University of Maryland Law School.*

*6. -**Create a plan to see the entire world** and taste it   slowly.*

*7. -**Write songs** and other musical pieces.*

*8. -**Create a musical.** (which is now in progress.)*

*9. -**And on, and on,** and on,*

UNTIL...!

You see, there was no one telling me what I should or shouldn't do. I had total freedom and this total freedom is so sweet. Sweeter than all the ice cream in the world!

And of course,

I DO ONLY WHAT I LOVE TO DO.

When I calculate the time it would take for me to experience all my projects, I figured I would have to live to be 137 ½ years old. I added the half year just in case I'd made a mathematical error. You can see I gave myself plenty of room. It was very important to do so.

Andrew

But for right now, it is very important for me to eat some peanuts. I prefer them not cooked, roasted, or salted, ...plain and raw.

An Answer:

I go

to those who feed

My Soul

and

Question

Their Soul Food.

An Answer:

Doing

what

I Love

to Do

Brings Me

Beautiful Peace.

Do

I

Appreciate

My

Life?

*Life requires Question # **13***

"Do I Appreciate My Life ?"

YES !   IN FACT, I LOVE IT...!!!

I feel extremely fortunate, and I value every minute.

I respect everything.

I am doing only what I love to do.

I cherish every encounter.

I am grateful for my friends, my pets, my world, my universe, and everyone who comes and goes by me. By the way, all ...yes all... of my relatives and teachers are my friends.

I am grateful for farmers and especially the people who gather the fruits and vegetables. The gatherers perform such a great service, and yet they receive so little economic rewards.

I am grateful for the "Black Walnut Trees".
(Their nuts provide great food and nourishment for me.)

I am grateful for the companies and the people who make my ice cream.

I am grateful for everything.

Andrew

And today, I can hardly wait, for my freshly baked Coconut Custard Pie, ...with a glass of milk.

An Answer:

*I prefer
impossible dreams.*

They get rid of

nightmares.

An Answer:

This Planet
Understands
and
Provides
what Humans Need.

Question 14

Do I Choose Healthy or Unhealthy Reactions?

*The result of every action is Question # **14***

"Do I choose Healthy or Unhealthy Reactions?"

Oh!   This one! Yes, this one still has power over me until I realize what is happening. Sometimes, it takes several minutes for me to recognize I am choosing unhealthy reactions.

One of my better examples is this:

One day, a long time ago, I was in a hurry to leave home to go to work. The first thing I noticed was the front tire on my car was flat. I became so angry that I kicked the tire with all my anger. And guess what?...I hurt my big toe so badly that I went limping home to call my office to tell them I would be late.

I remember sitting in a chair, my big toe throbbing, and saying to myself, "Andrew, how stupid you can be!" What did I accomplish by creating this action? A lot of pain. This pain was so unnecessary and not very smart.

So, I decided right then and there, in the future, to change my attitude to:
"Well ...I guess I need the exercise right now, so change the tire now and ...choose to do it peacefully."

I am sure most of us prefer to be healthy, and it appears most of us love to be nourished. We think, feel, and act healthier when we eat food that is healthy for us. We understand this. However, it appears to me many of us are not aware of how destructive thoughts act upon our minds, bodies, and spirit. And a terrible fact is...

Destructive people not only are dangerous to themselves, but also to their families, friends, and anyone with whom they share any kind of relationship.
The world also suffers.

Many of us would not walk toward a poisonous snake; in fact, I would run away. Yet most of us do not see, hear, or feel the danger of destructive people until it is too late.
And then, Bam! ....They give it to us.

Some of our children are still being taught destructive behavior
and
it affects every one of us.

We can't walk the streets safely. We have to lock our doors. We're frightened by unusual or strange noises, and I have to carry too many keys now. I don't know about you, but I am tired of carrying so many keys. It doesn't have to be this way, does it?

There is always, always, always a healthier way.

Road rage is an epidemic we face almost daily. I have trained myself to choose a healthy reaction by saying to myself, "That's interesting, pay attention to the road."
Or I say, "That person is probably having a rough day, or they're probably sick today. Do not pay any attention to their behavior, keep your mind on your job. Pay attention to the road, do not join their sickness. Simply choose to react in a healthy manner."

I try not to choose a reaction with anger. I try to choose a reaction in a healthy manner, with peace. By choosing healthy reactions, I can be happier, healthier, and wealthier in all ways.
  Andrew Jennings

Right now, I am choosing to go to my gym. I am becoming better every month! I can now do 122 sit-ups, 131 push-ups, and 100 jump-rope-swings!
..... No ice cream today. Tomorrow will be the day.
..... Huckleberry Ice Cream!

An Answer:

I create My World,

I create My Stress,

by...HOW

I create

MY THOUGHTS

An Answer:

I focus on what is really important in life

Reason

rather

than

Rules.

Question 15

Do
I
Create
or
Imitate?

Creation likes Question # 15

" Do I Create or Imitate? "

"The Book of Proverbs" has instructed me to use much counsel. It appears to me it is to my benefit to listen very, very carefully and take what I consider the best idea for my purposes. However, I think it practical for me to consider the perceptions of others and consider my idea might be or not be valid.

No two of us will dress alike, look alike, act alike, be balanced alike, think alike and feel alike. Some of us will look at the situation with thick glasses, some will have thin glasses, and others might be somewhere in between. Especially, we do not choose our ice cream alike: look at all the different flavors!

However, I feel as if I must bring together all facts brought forth, and I must remind myself that facts are very stubborn things, and feelings are not always facts.

I go deep inside of myself and listen to what I say because it is my life, my joys, my interests, my explorations, my dreams, my hopes. No one will listen to me as carefully as I do.

The creative forces of life have given me the great gift of creating myself, and the instant I understood and acknowledged this fact, I felt an overwhelming feeling of being very, very expansive, because I can create new discoveries just by altering my attitudes and thoughts or by making different choices.

When I imitate, it means the great gift I have, will never be shown. I will never share the truth of "Who I Am" with my fellow beings and with myself. This may mean I will never experience the feelings of being criticized for the truth ...never allowing the truth to enter my being.

I have heard it said:

"IMITATION IS THE GREATEST FLATTERY"

I don't know about you, but I am not interested in being flattered. I always welcome any form of criticism, positive or negative, but not insincere praise.

An apple tree does not produce pears, and an orange tree does not produce peaches. We come from a highly developed creative center. We are not apples, pears, oranges, or peaches.

WE ARE A

HIGHLY DEVELOPED CREATIVE FORCE

CREATED BY

A HIGHLY DEVELOPED CREATIVE FORCE

NAMED HUMAN BEINGS.

No one walks, talks, looks, eats, sleeps, thinks, emotes, or acts the same way as I do. And all of my friends are always thanking God for this!

I have read that imitation can be a slow suicide.

I don't know about a "slow suicide," but I do know I prefer to create rather than imitate. I think to create can be more interesting and funnier.

                              Andrew

But it's not funny.....
        that I love Coconut Custard Pie so much,
        .....and Ice Cream soooooo much !!!

An Answer:

*Negative and
Destructive
Emotions*

such as

*Anger, Jealousy and
Hatred,*

*Create Unhappy
Cells.*

An Answer:

Wisdom

Seeks

Questions!

Question 16

Do
I
Live
in
Harmony
or
Disharmony?

Beauty is found in Question # 16

"Do I Live in Harmony or Disharmony?

I have often meditated on the following phrase:

"THE PEACE THAT PASSES ALL UNDERSTANDING"

I have wondered how to achieve this kind of peace.
I have considered the fact that if any one human being can acquire this great peace, isn't it also possible for me to acquire the same feeling?

OF COURSE IT IS !

I know when I choose to turn left, I could just as easily choose to turn right. And when I choose to take the road having thorns and briars of anxiety, discord, or discomfort, I also can choose to take the road leading me toward Peace, Joy and Harmony.

IT IS ALWAYS MY CHOICE !

Depending on where I am, the road to peace depends on my choice: the discipline to maintain a steady direction or the discipline to control my thoughts until I know without a doubt I can move in the direction I desire.

There may be many negative destructive movements in my journey, but with a strong determination, a lot of practice with patience, a lot of keeping my focus and guiding my being.

I AM ON THE ROAD OF CHOICES LEADING ME TO

"THE PEACE THAT PASSES ALL UNDERSTANDING."

<u>*PEACE*</u>

<u>*THAT CREATES ALL BEAUTIFUL HARMONIES.*</u>

One of my dictionaries has harmonic expressions for the word
HARMONY :
    1. Getting along well together

    2. Agreement of feelings, ideas, or actions

    3. A pleasing arrangement of parts

    4. A sweet musical sound

Other dictionaries define HARMONY as
Unity, friendship, balance, togetherness, rapport, closeness, compatible, in tune, complementary, blending, peaceful.

DISHARMONY definitions include:
    1. Not getting along well together

    2. Disagreement of feelings, ideas, or actions

    3. An unpleasant arrangement

    4. An unpleasant musical sound

    5. Discord

    6. Dissonance

    7. A doomed project

    8. Incompatible

    9. Out of tune

    10. Out of balance

And the beautiful harmonic structures of my orange and banana are going to make my cells happy today!

An Answer:

Opinions

have many different

Flavors.

An Answer:

Facts

are

very

Stubborn

Things.

Do

I

Encourage

or

Discourage?

The importance of courage is Question # 17

"Do I Encourage or Discourage?"

When I analyzed the words "ENCOURAGE" and "DISCOURAGE", I discovered the last two syllables have the same spelling and have the same meaning.
Interesting, isn't it?

The word is COURAGE, and many times in my life, I wished I had more of it.

I always

ENCOURAGE

because it raises the spirit,

gives confidence,

and

produces more creativity.

It never enters my mind to discourage anyone from anything that is healthy. It is just not the right thing to do. After many years of practicing encouragement on myself,

It becomes easier each year,
and I'm still practicing . I love it!

Andrew

Good, Old' Sassafras Tea, is great for me today. It makes all my cells very happy. And if there is one thing I have learned, ...it is...

to keep my cells happy!

An Answer:

With

Answers

...Fears Leave.

An Answer:

And...

Someone You know

may be waiting

to discover

The Answers.

Do I

Accept

or

Reject

Responsibility

for

My Actions?

My actions create Question # 18

"Do I Accept or Reject Responsibility for My Actions?"

Some of the excuses I have heard in life are so funny :

"The Devil made me do it."

I laugh every time I hear this. The poor old devil is blamed for almost everything, and I am sure he doesn't know anything about these accusations.

Perhaps I shouldn't laugh when I hear:

" My mother's genes ...made me do it."
"My teacher ...made me do it."
"My grandparents ...made me do it."
"My culture ...made me do it."
"They ...made me do it"

I laugh quietly.

I have never been able to discover who THEY ARE,

but I guess THEY KNOW!

For me, I always accept the responsibility for my actions.

It is healthier in all areas to admit an error as it is. The situation moves faster and gives me my freedom.

Andrew J.

And I move very fast when I get a new shipment of Black Walnuts.

An Answer:

Many say they have the

Right Answers,

but

Questions

will determine who has

The Truth

An Answer:

Ignorance

avoids

Questions

because

Answers

expose

The Truth.

Question 19

How
Much
Have I
Learned?

*All matters of education calls for Question # **19**.*

"How much have I learned?"

Not

Enough !

However, I feel as if I have been extremely fortunate to have had so many chances and so many choices to learn what I wanted to learn. And yet, with hundreds of chances and hundreds of choices,

> *I would like to go further in feeling the beauty of being more aware in all areas.*

Learning has made possible the clearest path to rid me of my fears and allow me to be free. Yes, freedom is a great learning experience.

> *Persistence sprinkled with patience and humor is extremely healthy for me.*
>
> Andrew J.

Did you know that cashews and bananas together taste soooo good?

I just learned that!

An Answer:

I

enjoy

my own

company,

and...

I am never alone!

An Answer:

CHANGE

IS

the *most*

Constant

THING

of

everything!

Question 20

How Much
Have
I
Loved?

Not

Enough!

How About You...?

An Answer:

Love

is a

Nourishment

to

Oneself

or to

Another.

An Answer:

And the

A n s w e r s

will change

as ...

I C h a n g e

Question 21

How
Do
I
Feel ?

I FEEL GOOD !

So good, in fact,

that all the
Ice cream, Black Walnuts, Peaches, Blueberries,
Huckleberries, Raw Peanuts, Watermelons, Oranges,
in the World could not bring me
Greater Joy!

FORTY-THREE YEARS AGO,

I STARTED THIS PROJECT.

But I figure this isn't so bad.
The most important thing is the fact that I finished, I
completed the work, and I said to myself,

"It is now finished ...UNTIL!"
It has taught me to have
Greater Persistence,
Greater Patience,
Greater Humor
than I ever imagined.

THE JOY OF COMPLETION

creates a great

" PEACE THAT PASSES ALL UNDERSTANDING"

and to

APPRECIATE

The Magic and Beauty of Everything!!!

An Answer:

Feelings are Messages.

and...

Messages are Feelings.

An Answer:

I feel a Freedom

that passes all

Knowledge.

An Answer:

Feelings

are an

Energy

which can move

The Intelligence

forward, overcoming

Many Obstacles.

At this point,

I want

to remind you,

that the Answers

that I have presented,

are only Answers

that have satisfied me.

The roads you take

will be different.

And this alone

will guide you to

different Answers.

This is Your Book.

*Share it with someone
and,
the best of all,
give it to someone
you love,
or perhaps someone
you don't love,
or just anyone
you know
or
don't know.*

And don't forget:

Someone may be waiting to discover

The Answers!

Don't forget:

The

Best Way

to

predict

Your Future

is to

Create It.

" *The*

Question

Is more Important

than the

Answer"

Socrates...Born 469 B.C.

Plato... Born 428 B.C.

I hope you liked this Book.

Andrew Jennings Dickerson

<u>ABOUT THE AUTHOR:</u>

The following comments are from the Author's daughter, Andra Lee Beames:

He has been the greatest father a girl could have! He has been my drummer for all my life (and thank God) he has rhythm!!!

He has been an educator, an officer in the military, a musician, involved with many types of businesses (usually the president). At his age 50, I witnessed his musical growth of majoring in musical performance of classical piano and classical trombone. He had decided: "Now is the time".

He gave me my first piano and automobile driving lessons. His love of traveling took Mom, my three sisters, Lou-Ann, Margie and Porter, across the United States, 4 to 6 weeks in the summer. From Delaware to California, he found places we could swim every day. It was exciting traveling the mountains in Mexico.

He has performed many years with my family's band "The Pickin Hats" traveling in many states and Canada. With the "Keili Kids" our family performed in Ireland and on BBC.

Having many projects to finish, he told me, he had to live at least 137 ½ years! One of his better projects is a Broadway musical titled "Babies and Birthdays" creating the music, lyrics and book. Another project is writing a series of 21 books about magnificent subjects.

He has accomplished several projects already, finding ways to be happy, acquiring great peace, and loving the life he lives.

He took my children Sam and Sarah to breakfast almost every Sunday and discussed the "Magnificent Questions" with them. It was the highlight of their week.

I feel my Dad has written an "old fashioned charming book". Informing everyone when we choose a nourishing life for ourselves, we are also choosing a nourishing life for everyone, including this Planet.

I hope you like it!

Andra Lee Beames

Dear Reader:

If you have a question, a comment or an answer, please let me know. Being a collector of attitudes I will welcome the opportunity to learn and to share.

Thank you,
Andrew Jennings Dickerson

<u>*Coming up:*</u>
        " Magnificent Attitudes"

        "Magnificent Teachers"

        "Magnificent Philosophies"

Web Site:

w.w.w. Collector Of Attitudes.com